DOUGLAS ASANTE

FAITH ON FIRE

IDENTITY

A Devotional for Youth

——— VOLUME **ONE** ———

•JAN •FEB •MAR

FAITH ON FIRE – VOLUME 1: IDENTITY
A Devotional for Youth

Copyright © 2025 Equip Publishing House Ltd

ISBN: 978-1-916692-46-6

Scripture quotations are taken from The Holy Bible, New International Version® (NIV), New Living Translation® (NLT), and other public domain translations, where indicated.

Published by **Equip Publishing House Ltd**
Accra, Ghana | London, UK

Printed in the United Kingdom.

DEDICATION

To every young person who's ever wondered, *"Who am I, really?"*

You are seen. You are chosen. You are loved beyond measure.

May these words remind you that your identity in Christ is unshakeable — no matter what life throws your way.

ACKNOWLEDGEMENTS

To the amazing youth who inspire these pages — your courage, honesty, and questions keep faith alive and real. To our youth leaders, parents, and mentors — thank you for believing in the next generation.

And above all, to Jesus — the fire that never goes out.

FOREWORD

In a world that constantly tells young people who they should be, *Faith on Fire* is a call back to who God says they already are.

Volume 1: *Identity* takes you on a 90-day journey to rediscover your true worth — not in likes, grades, or popularity, but in Christ.

Each day offers a simple rhythm: a verse to reflect on, a real story to connect with, a short insight, and a challenge to live out your faith.

It's not about perfection; it's about growing closer to God, one step at a time.

Take a deep breath.

You don't need to have it all figured out.

Just start — one day, one verse, one prayer at a time.

You were made for this fire.

NOTE TO PARENTS & YOUTH LEADERS

Dear Parents, Mentors, and Youth Leaders,

Thank you for investing in the hearts of young people. *Faith on Fire* was written to help the next generation discover who they are in Christ — confidently, passionately, and personally.

This devotional is designed to be flexible — it can be used **individually**, in **small groups**, or as part of a **youth ministry journey**. Each day's reflection connects real stories with biblical truth in a way that's relatable and practical for teenagers and young adults (ages 13–21).

Here are a few ideas to help guide them along the way:

Encourage Consistency, Not Perfection.

Life gets busy, but remind them that faith isn't a checklist — it's a relationship. Missing a day doesn't mean they've failed; it's just a moment to start again.

Create Safe Spaces For Honesty.

Invite real conversations. Let questions be asked — even the hard ones. God meets us in our curiosity and our doubts.

Use The Journal Prompts For Group Discussions.

These questions make powerful tools for reflection circles or cell group meetings. Encourage open sharing without judgement.

Model What Faith Looks Like.

Teens don't just listen to words — they watch lives. Let them see what grace, patience, and humility look like in action.

Pray Over Them.

Even when you don't know what to say, prayer has power. Ask God to keep their hearts burning bright with faith that lasts.

Thank you for walking beside this generation as they learn to walk with God for themselves.

May the fire of faith begin in their hearts — and spread to everyone around them.

With gratitude,

Douglas
Rev Minister and Author

INTRODUCTION

There's something powerful about fire — it spreads, it shines, it transforms.

When faith comes alive in your heart, it lights up every part of your life. That's what this devotional is about — discovering who you are in Christ and letting that truth burn bright.

Over the next three months, you'll walk through three themes:

JANUARY — **Who You Are in Christ**
FEBRUARY — **Faith in Motion**
MARCH — **Living Set Apart**

You'll see how God sees you, learn to live with purpose, and grow the kind of faith that changes everything.

Don't rush through. Take time to pray, write, and listen. Your journal entries matter. Your story matters. Because you matter to God.

HOW TO USE THIS DEVOTIONAL

Faith on Fire isn't just another book to read — it's a journey to experience.

Think of it as a daily conversation with God. Each page is designed to help you grow stronger in your faith, understand who you are in Christ, and live it out in real life.

Here's how to get the most out of it:

1. Find Your Quiet Space.

Start or end your day in a calm place — no distractions, no pressure. Just you and God.

2. Read the Key Verse slowly.

Don't rush. Let the words sink in. Try reading it out loud or writing it down in your notebook.

3. Connect with the Story.

Every devotional begins with a real-life story. Imagine yourself in it — what would you do? How does it relate to your world?

4. Reflect on the Insight.

This is where truth meets you personally. Think about what God might be saying to you today.

5. Take the Action Step seriously.

Faith isn't just something you believe — it's something you live. Try the challenge. See what happens.

6. END WITH THE PRAYER.

Make it your own. Add your thoughts, emotions, and questions. God loves hearing from you — just as you are.

7. WRITE IN THE JOURNAL PROMPT SECTION.

Don't skip this! Journalling helps you process what you're learning. Be honest. Be bold. Be you.

Remember: this isn't about perfection — it's about progress.

You don't have to do it *every* day in a row. If you miss one, just pick up where you left off. God's not keeping score — He's walking with you.

A BLESSING FOR THE READER

Father,

Thank You for this young person holding this book.

You know their heart, their dreams, their fears, and their story.

As they read these pages, may Your voice grow louder than the noise of the world.

Remind them daily that they are chosen, loved, and set apart for something great.

Let their faith burn brighter with each word they read.

When they feel weak, be their strength.

When they feel lost, be their guide.

When they doubt, remind them — *they belong to You.*

May their life shine so brightly that others see You in them.

In Jesus' name,

Amen.

January

WHO YOU ARE
IN CHRIST

You're Not an Accident

"Before I formed you in the womb
I knew you, before you were
born I set you apart."

JEREMIAH 1:5 (NIV)

STORY

Leah sometimes felt invisible. Her parents were always arguing, her grades hovered in the middle, and her friends seemed to forget she existed.

One night, feeling completely unseen, she scrolled through her phone and stopped at a verse someone had posted: *Jeremiah 1:5.*

She read it once, then again. *"Before I formed you... I knew you."*

It hit her — God had known her before anyone else did.

She wasn't a mistake in a noisy world; she was part of a plan that started in God's heart.

INSIGHT

You're not random.

You're not the result of chance or bad timing.

God thought about you, dreamed about you, and made you on purpose.

Even when you feel forgotten, He hasn't moved an inch away.

He sees you, knows your name, and calls you His own.

> *"You were in God's plan before
> you were in your parents' arms."*

ACTION STEP

Write this truth somewhere you'll see it often:

"God made me on purpose, for a purpose."

Read it every morning this week.

PRAYER

God, thank You for creating me with care. Help me to believe that my life matters because You designed it. When I feel invisible, remind me that You see me. Amen.

JOURNAL PROMPT

When do you feel most unseen or forgotten?

What does it mean to you that God already knew you — completely — before you were born?

Chosen, Not Forgotten

*"For he chose us in him before
the creation of the world to be holy
and blameless in his sight."*

EPHESIANS 1:4 (NIV)

STORY

Marcus was used to being left out.

He wasn't the loudest or the most talented, so when football teams were picked, he was usually one of the last names called.

It made him wonder if he'd ever really fit anywhere.

Then one day at youth group, the speaker read Ephesians 1:4 and said, "Before the world even began, God chose you."

Marcus couldn't stop thinking about that. *Before the world began?* That meant before any rejection, failure, or opinion — God already wanted him.

Insight

You've never been an afterthought.

Even when people overlook you, God never has.

He chose you before you had achievements, friends, or a name.
His choice wasn't based on your performance but on His love.

That means you can rest — you already belong.

> ## *"You were handpicked by God long before you felt left out by anyone."*

Action Step

Every time you feel excluded this week, remind yourself: "I was chosen before anyone else even knew me."

Prayer

God, thank You for choosing me long before I could ever earn it.

Help me to live confident in that truth — that I'm Yours. Amen.

Journal Prompt

When was the last time you felt overlooked?

What does it mean that God saw and chose you before the world even started?

Loved Without Conditions

*"Nothing can ever separate us
from God's love.*

ROMANS 8:38-39 (NLT)

STORY

Naomi felt far from God.

She hadn't prayed in weeks, skipped church a few times, and assumed God must be disappointed.

Scrolling one night, she saw a post: *"God doesn't love you less when you mess up."*

She rolled her eyes — until she read Romans 8:38-39.

Could it really be true that nothing could separate her from His love?

That night she whispered, "Even me?"

And somehow, she knew the answer was yes.

Insight

God's love isn't a reward — it's a promise.

It doesn't shrink when you fail or grow when you do better.

He loves you the same on your worst day as He does on your best.

When guilt says, "You blew it," grace whispers, "You're still mine."

> *"God's love doesn't come with small print or expiry dates."*

Action Step

Take a moment today to thank God for loving you as you are — no pretending, no pressure.

Prayer

Lord, thank You for loving me even when I don't deserve it.

Help me rest in Your love and not run from it. Amen.

Journal Prompt

Where do you struggle to believe God still loves you? Write how His love meets you right there.

God Doesn't Make Mistakes

"I praise you because I am fearfully and wonderfully made."

PSALM 139:14 (NIV)

STORY

Aaron spent years wishing he was someone else — smarter, taller, funnier, better.

He looked at his friends and thought, *"Why can't I be like them?"*

Then one night at youth group, the leader read Psalm 139 and said, "When God made you, He didn't mess up."

Aaron laughed under his breath, but the words stuck.

Maybe God really had a plan when He gave him his laugh, his quirks, his quiet heart.

He didn't need to be a copy of anyone — God made him an original.

INSIGHT

You weren't built by accident.

Every detail of who you are — your personality, your voice, your way of thinking — was designed on purpose.

When you compare yourself to others, you question God's design.

But He doesn't make mistakes.

> *"The Creator of galaxies*
> *also handcrafted you*
> *— perfectly on purpose."*

ACTION STEP

Look in the mirror today and thank God for one thing about yourself that makes you unique.

PRAYER

Father, thank You for creating me with care.

Help me to stop comparing and start celebrating how You made me. Amen.

JOURNAL PROMPT

What's one part of yourself you've struggled to accept?

How could God use that very thing for something good?

Fearfully and Wonderfully Made

"For you created my inmost being;
you knit me together
in my mother's womb."

PSALM 139:13 (NIV)

STORY

Maya spent hours comparing herself to people online.

Everyone looked happier, prettier, more confident.

She started thinking, *Maybe I'm just ordinary.*

Then during Bible study, she read Psalm 139 and paused: *"You knit me together."*

It sounded so personal — like God had taken His time.

That night, she realised she wasn't a mistake; she was a masterpiece.

INSIGHT

You are not "just another person."

You are a work of art made by the greatest Artist.

God designed you with detail, love, and purpose.

You don't need to fit into the world's version of perfect — God already calls you wonderful.

> *"You're not mass-produced.*
> *You're hand-crafted by God."*

ACTION STEP

Say this out loud: "God made me wonderful."

Repeat it until your heart starts to believe it.

PRAYER

Lord, thank You for making me exactly how You wanted.

Help me to see myself through Your eyes. Amen.

JOURNAL PROMPT

What's one thing about yourself — inside or out — that you can thank God for today?

You Belong Here

"Now you are the body of Christ,
and each one of you is a part of it."

1 CORINTHIANS 12:27 (NIV)

STORY

Jordan felt like the odd one out at church.

Everyone seemed to have their place — the singers, the speakers, the confident ones.

He loved God but never felt he fit in anywhere.

Then one Sunday, his youth pastor said, "You don't need to be like everyone else to belong — you belong because you're part of the body."

Something clicked.

If the church is like a body, maybe he wasn't the leftover part — maybe he was a piece that made it complete.

INSIGHT

You belong — not because you're perfect or popular, but because God says you do.

In His family, everyone has a place.

You're not extra, forgotten, or unneeded.
You have gifts only you can bring, and when you use them, the body becomes whole.

> *"You're not a spare part —
> you're a vital piece of God's plan."*

ACTION STEP

Find one way to contribute this week — help someone, serve at church, or encourage a friend.

PRAYER

God, thank You that I belong in Your family.

Show me how to use what You've given me to make a difference. Amen.

JOURNAL PROMPT

Where do you feel most left out?

How might God be showing you that you already belong?

Seen and Known

*"You have searched me,
Lord, and you know me."*

PSALM 139:1 (NIV)

STORY

Amira didn't like crowds. In big groups she felt invisible — like no one noticed her or cared what she thought.

During youth worship one evening, the leader read Psalm 139 and said, "God doesn't just see you; He knows you."

That line landed hard. God knew her thoughts, her fears, her dreams — everything.

For the first time, she realised that being known by God mattered more than being noticed by people.

INSIGHT

You don't need to fight for attention when you already have God's full focus.

He knows every detail — your heartbeat, your struggles, your hopes.

You are fully seen and deeply loved, even when no one else claps for you.

> *"You're never invisible
> to the One who made you."*

ACTION STEP

Take five quiet minutes today and talk to God honestly about how you feel. He's already listening.

PRAYER

Lord, thank You for seeing me when I feel unseen.

Help me to rest in the fact that You know me completely and still love me. Amen.

JOURNAL PROMPT

What would you say to God if you knew He was really listening right now?

You Have a Voice

*"Don't let anyone look down
on you because you are young,
but set an example for the believers."*

1 TIMOTHY 4:12 (NIV)

STORY

Elijah was quiet — not shy, just unsure his opinions mattered.

He'd sit in youth group with great ideas but never speak up.

Then one night his leader said, "Your voice could be the encouragement someone's waiting for."

That week, Elijah prayed before school and felt nudged to encourage a friend who was down.

It was small, but it mattered — and he realised his voice could make a difference.

Insight

Your age doesn't disqualify you.

God has put something inside you that this world needs — courage, kindness, truth, creativity.

When you stay silent, the world misses out.

Speak with love, live with boldness, and let your words bring light.

> *"You don't need a microphone to make an impact — just courage to use your voice."*

Action Step

Say one encouraging thing to someone today — a friend, teacher, or family member.

Prayer

God, thank You for giving me a voice.
Help me to use it wisely to encourage and bring hope.
Amen.

Journal Prompt

When's a time you wanted to speak up but didn't? What held you back?

Stand Firm

"Be on your guard;
stand firm in the faith;
be courageous; be strong."

1 CORINTHIANS 16:13 (NIV)

STORY

Ruben didn't like confrontation, so when his friends mocked his faith, he laughed it off.

But later, he felt uneasy.

He wanted to fit in — but not at the cost of what he believed.

At youth group, his leader shared this verse and said, "Courage isn't about being loud — it's about staying true."

That hit home.

Ruben decided to stop hiding his faith. Next time his friends joked, he didn't argue — he just smiled and stood firm.

Insight

It's not easy to stand for truth in a world that bends it.

But strength isn't about shouting; it's about staying steady when others shift.

You might lose approval, but you'll gain peace — and God will back your courage.

> *"Stand firm, even if you stand alone —*
> *God stands with you."*

Action Step

Ask God for courage to be real about your faith this week, even in small ways.

Prayer

Lord, help me to stand strong in who You are and who I am in You. Amen.

Journal Prompt

Where are you tempted to compromise your faith?

What would standing firm look like there?

Mirror Truths

"Anyone who belongs to Christ
has become a new person.
The old life is gone; a new life has begun!"

2 CORINTHIANS 5:17 (NLT)

STORY

Ella struggled to like herself.

She'd made mistakes and couldn't forget them —
every time she looked in the mirror, she saw who
she used to be.

One Sunday, her youth leader said, "God doesn't see
who you were; He sees who you're becoming."

That night, she looked at her reflection again —
this time as someone forgiven.

Same face, new heart.

INSIGHT

The mirror shows your face, not your future.

If you're in Christ, you're not defined by what you've done — you're defined by what He's done for you.

The old you is gone. The new you is learning to live free.

> *"Don't believe everything the mirror says — believe what God says."*

ACTION STEP

Write down one thing you've been forgiven for and thank God for a fresh start.

PRAYER

Jesus, thank You for making me new.
Help me see myself the way You do — forgiven and loved.
Amen.

JOURNAL PROMPT

What old labels or mistakes do you need to let go of today?

Confidence in Christ

"The Lord will be your confidence."

PROVERBS 3:26 (NKJV)

STORY

Kofi used to walk into class comparing himself to everyone else — who was smarter, cooler, more confident.

He pretended not to care, but inside he felt small.

Then his cousin told him, "Confidence doesn't come from being the best — it comes from knowing Whose you are."

That night, Kofi prayed differently.

Instead of asking to be better, he thanked God for being with him.

The next morning, he didn't try to impress anyone — he just walked in as himself.

Insight

Confidence isn't arrogance. It's knowing that God is with you, so you don't have to prove yourself.

When you walk with Him, you don't need to fake strength — you borrow His.

True confidence starts with trust, not perfection.

> ## *"Real confidence is quiet — it knows God's got this."*

Action Step

Before you start your day, whisper this: "God, be my confidence today."

Prayer

Lord, help me walk with quiet confidence, trusting that You're enough — and so am I in You. Amen.

Journal Prompt

Where do you need more confidence? How could trusting God change the way you approach it?

January

God's Got a Plan

"'For I know the plans I have for you,'
declares the Lord, 'plans to prosper
you and not to harm you, plans
to give you hope and a future.'"

JEREMIAH 29:11 (NIV)

STORY

Zara hated not knowing what came next.

She worried about exams, her future, and what she'd do with her life. Everyone else seemed sure about their path — except her.

Then one morning she read Jeremiah 29:11. It didn't fix everything, but it made her breathe again.

If God had a plan, maybe she didn't need to have every answer.

Maybe trusting Him meant letting go of control and walking one step at a time.

Insight

You don't need to have your whole life figured out —
God already does.

His plan isn't a mystery to Him, only to us.

You can rest knowing His timing is perfect and His
purpose will stand.

> *"You don't need to see
> the whole map when you
> know the One who made it."*

Action Step

Write down one area of your life you're worried about.
Pray and give it back to God today.

Prayer

Lord, thank You that You already know what's next.
Help me trust Your plan even when I can't see it.
Amen.

Journal Prompt

Where do you find it hardest to trust God's plan
right now?

Purpose in Progress

*"Being confident of this, that he who
began a good work in you
will carry it on to completion."*

PHILIPPIANS 1:6 (NIV)

STORY

Amos hated feeling "not there yet."

He wanted to be mature, spiritual, strong — but
he still struggled.

One day at youth group, someone said, "You're not
failing; you're forming."

Those words stuck. God wasn't done with him —
He was still working.

Now, every time Amos feels impatient with himself,
he remembers: progress beats perfection.

Insight

God's not expecting you to be finished — He's shaping you.

He's patient, gentle, and fully committed to your growth.

You might not see it daily, but change is happening inside you.

Don't give up just because you're not there yet.

> *"God's not finished — He's just getting started with you."*

Action Step

Write a short thank-you prayer for how far you've come, even if you're still growing.

Prayer

Lord, thank You that You're still working in me.
Help me trust the process and not rush what You're building. Amen.

Journal Prompt

Where can you see signs of growth in your faith, even if it's small?

Guard Your Mind

*"Do not conform to the pattern
of this world, but be transformed
by the renewing of your mind."*

ROMANS 12:2 (NIV)

STORY

Kayla realised how much her thoughts shaped
her mood.

When she scrolled too long, she felt anxious. When
she compared herself, she felt low.

At church, her youth pastor said, "What you feed
your mind shapes your life."

So she started swapping some scrolling time for
worship music and short devotionals.

Slowly, peace replaced pressure.

Insight

Your mind is like a garden — what you plant grows.

If you fill it with truth, peace blooms. If you feed it lies, weeds spread.

God wants to renew how you think so you can live with joy and purpose.

> *"You can't have a peaceful life with a cluttered mind."*

Action Step

Take a short break from social media today. Use that time to read one encouraging verse instead.

Prayer

God, help me protect what I let into my mind. Teach me to focus on what's true and life-giving. Amen.

Journal Prompt

What thoughts tend to pull you down?

What truth from God could replace them?

Gratitude Changes Everything

*"Give thanks in all circumstances;
for this is God's will for you
in Christ Jesus."*

1 THESSALONIANS 5:18 (NIV)

STORY

Joel had been in a bad mood all week.

Everything felt stressful — deadlines, friends, even church.

Then his mum challenged him: "Say three things you're grateful for before bed."

It felt silly at first, but after a few nights, he noticed something — his attitude changed.

The problems didn't vanish, but gratitude made room for peace.

INSIGHT

Thankfulness doesn't ignore problems; it changes your perspective.

When you focus on what's good, you give less space to what's wrong.

Gratitude isn't just a feeling — it's a choice that opens the door to joy.

> *"Gratitude doesn't change your situation — it changes you."*

ACTION STEP

Write down three things you're grateful for today — big or small — and thank God for them.

PRAYER

Lord, thank You for all the blessings I often forget.

Help me to live thankful, even when life feels tough. Amen.

JOURNAL PROMPT

What's one thing you can thank God for today that you've taken for granted?

Waiting Well

"Those who hope in the Lord will renew their strength."

ISAIAH 40:31 (NIV)

STORY

Ella prayed for something for months — and nothing seemed to happen.

She started wondering if God was even listening.

One evening, she read Isaiah 40:31 and realised waiting wasn't wasted time — it was growing time.

Maybe God wasn't saying "no"; maybe He was saying "not yet."

And maybe, just maybe, the waiting was building her strength.

Insight

Waiting isn't punishment — it's preparation.

God uses delays to shape your faith, not to discourage it.

He's never late; He's just teaching you to trust His timing.

> *"If God's making you wait,*
> *He's building something*
> *worth the wait."*

Action Step

Think of one thing you're waiting on. Ask God for patience, not just answers.

Prayer

God, help me to trust You while I wait.

Renew my strength and remind me You're working, even when I can't see it. Amen.

Journal Prompt

What's something you've been waiting for? How could God be using this time to prepare you?

Faith Over Feelings

"We live by faith, not by sight."

2 CORINTHIANS 5:7 (NIV)

STORY

Talia had been praying for something big — and nothing was changing.

Every time she looked around, it felt like God was silent.

She started wondering if her prayers were even heard.

But one night during worship, the lyrics said, *"Even when I don't see it, You're working."*

Tears filled her eyes. Maybe faith wasn't about seeing; maybe it was about trusting.

INSIGHT

Faith isn't a feeling — it's a choice.

Your emotions go up and down, but God's truth stays steady.

Even when you don't *feel* close to God, He's closer than you think.

Faith says, "I'll believe it, even when I don't see it yet."

> ## "Feelings change — faith chooses to trust anyway."

ACTION STEP

Every time you feel discouraged today, say aloud: "God is still working."

PRAYER

God, help me trust You even when I don't see results. Remind me that You're faithful even when I don't feel it. Amen.

JOURNAL PROMPT

When was a time you felt far from God?

What helped you hold on?

Courage Over Fear

*"Be strong and courageous.
Do not be afraid; do not be
discouraged, for the Lord your God
will be with you wherever you go."*

JOSHUA 1:9 (NIV)

STORY

Owen was terrified of speaking in front of people.

When his teacher asked him to present a project, he almost said no.

That night, he read Joshua 1:9 and realised courage wasn't about being fearless — it was about trusting that God was with him.

He prayed, took a deep breath, and did it.

His hands shook, but he finished strong — and he knew he hadn't been alone.

INSIGHT

Courage doesn't mean you never feel afraid — it means you don't let fear stop you.

God's promise to be *with you* is bigger than whatever's against you.

You're not walking into anything alone.

> ## *"Fear whispers, 'What if?'*
> ## *God whispers, 'I'm with you.'"*

ACTION STEP

Do one small thing today that fear has been holding you back from.

PRAYER

Lord, help me remember You're always with me. Give me courage to do the things that scare me. Amen.

JOURNAL PROMPT

What fear is keeping you from moving forward?

How could courage look today?

See the Gold in People

"Love each other deeply.
Honour others above yourselves."

ROMANS 12:10 (NIV)

STORY

Sienna often rolled her eyes at people who annoyed her.

But one Sunday, her youth leader challenged everyone: "This week, find one good thing in everyone you meet."

It sounded impossible — until she tried it.

She noticed her quiet classmate was actually kind, and the loud boy in youth group was just nervous.

By the end of the week, Sienna realised something: people are easier to love when you look for the gold instead of the flaws.

Insight

It's easy to see what's wrong with people; it takes love to see what's right.

When you look through God's eyes, you'll find value where others see annoyance.

Honouring people doesn't make you weak — it shows strength and maturity.

> *"Look for gold, not dirt —*
> *you'll always find what*
> *you're searching for."*

Action Step

Say something kind about or to someone you've been judging lately.

Prayer

God, help me see people the way You see them — valuable, loved, and full of potential.
Amen.

Journal Prompt

Who's someone that's hard for you to love?

What's one positive thing you could recognise about them?

Watch Your Words

"The tongue has the power
of life and death."

PROVERBS 18:21 (NIV)

STORY

Noah liked to joke around, but sometimes his words crossed the line.

One day, a friend told him quietly, "That actually hurt."

He felt awful — he hadn't meant it that way.

Later, he read Proverbs 18:21 and realised how much power words carry.

He started being more intentional — using his words to build people up, not break them down.

Insight

Your words are powerful — they can bring healing or harm, hope or hurt.

Once spoken, they can't be taken back.

God wants your voice to be a source of life, not negativity.

When you speak, let your words sound like Jesus.

> *"Your words can plant peace*
> *or poison — choose wisely."*

Action Step

Encourage three people today. Use your words to bring life.

Prayer

Lord, help me speak words that lift others up, not tear them down. Teach me to pause before I speak. Amen.

Journal Prompt

Think of a time someone's words encouraged you.

How can you be that person for someone else?

Choose Light

"Let your light shine before others, that they may see your good deeds and glorify your Father in heaven."

MATTHEW 5:16 (NIV)

STORY

During a power cut, Maya's family lit a candle.

It was small, but it filled the room with light.

Her dad said, "See? Even a little light makes a big difference."

That moment stuck with her. Later, she realised it's the same with faith — even small acts of kindness can light up someone's darkness.

Insight

You don't need to be loud to shine — you just need to show up.

Your kindness, honesty, and love for people reflect Jesus more than you realise.

In a world full of darkness, one spark of light can change everything.

"You don't have to be the sun — just shine where you are."

Action Step

Do one small act of kindness today that brightens someone's day.

Prayer

Jesus, help me shine Your light wherever I go.

Let my life point people towards You. Amen.

Journal Prompt

Where can you bring light this week — at school, home, or online?

God is Closer Than You Think

"The Lord is near to all
who call on him."

PSALM 145:18 (NIV)

STORY

Jayden thought God was far away — somewhere in heaven, busy with "bigger" things.

When life got hard, he stopped praying because he figured God wasn't listening anyway.

Then one night, while listening to worship music, he felt something warm and peaceful in his chest. Not dramatic — just real.

It reminded him that God hadn't gone anywhere. He'd been there all along, waiting for him to notice.

Insight

God isn't distant — He's right beside you.

You don't have to shout for Him to hear or be perfect for Him to care.

When you whisper His name, He leans in. He's closer than your breath, nearer than your thoughts.

> *"When you can't feel God,*
> *trust that He still feels close."*

Action Step

Take five quiet minutes today to talk to God like He's right there — because He is.

Prayer

Lord, thank You for being near.

Help me to remember that I'm never alone, even when I don't feel You. Amen.

Journal Prompt

When was the last time you felt close to God?

What helped you sense His presence?

Forgiven and Free

"If we confess our sins,
he is faithful and just and
will forgive us our sins."

1 J O H N 1 : 9 (N I V)

STORY

Toby messed up. Big time.

He said something cruel to a friend and couldn't take it back. The guilt stuck with him for days.

Finally, he told his youth leader, who said, "God's not shocked by your mistake — He's ready to forgive it."

That night, Toby prayed honestly for the first time in ages.

He didn't feel instant fireworks, but he did feel lighter. Forgiven.

Insight

Guilt says, "You're finished." Grace says, "You're forgiven."

God's love isn't fragile — it can handle your worst day.

When you bring your mistakes to Him, He doesn't replay them; He releases them.

You don't need to stay trapped in shame — walk free.

> *"Your past may describe you,
> but it doesn't define you."*

Action Step

Be honest with God today about something you regret. Let Him remind you that forgiveness is yours.

Prayer

Jesus, thank You for forgiving me completely.

Help me forgive myself and live free from guilt. Amen.

Journal Prompt

What's something you've been holding onto that God has already forgiven?

Be the Reflection

*"Whoever claims to live in him
must live as Jesus did."*

1 JOHN 2:6 (NIV)

STORY

After youth group, Aria noticed how her leader
treated everyone — patient, kind, calm.

It wasn't fake; it was real. She thought, *I want my
faith to look like that.*

That week, she started making small changes —
listening more, being gentler, forgiving quicker.

She didn't become perfect, but people noticed the
difference.

She was starting to reflect Jesus.

INSIGHT

Faith isn't just about words — it's about reflection.

When people look at your life, do they see kindness, patience, and love?

You might be the only picture of Jesus someone ever sees. Let your actions reflect the One who changed you.

> *"When people see you,*
> *let them catch a glimpse of Him."*

ACTION STEP

Ask God to help you reflect His love in one situation today — especially where it's hard.

PRAYER

Jesus, help me be more like You in how I think, speak, and act.

Let my life reflect Your love. Amen.

JOURNAL PROMPT

Who in your life reflects Jesus well?

What can you learn from them?

The Company You Keep

*"Walk with the wise
and become wise, for a companion
of fools suffers harm."*

PROVERBS 13:20 (NIV)

STORY

Ethan started hanging out with a group that made bad choices.

He told himself he could handle it — until he realised he was changing too.

When his grades slipped and his temper grew, he knew something had to change.

He didn't cut everyone off, but he decided to spend more time with people who helped him grow instead of pull him down.

Insight

Your friends shape your future.

The people you hang around influence who you become — for better or worse.

Surround yourself with those who lift you, challenge you, and help you stay close to God.

> *"The right friends don't just hang out — they help you rise up."*

Action Step

Think about your closest friends. Are they helping or hindering your walk with God?

Pray about one friendship today.

Prayer

Lord, help me choose friends who push me closer to You, not away.

Teach me to be that kind of friend, too. Amen.

Journal Prompt

Who are three people who bring out the best in you — and why?

Faith in Action

"Do not merely listen to the word,
and so deceive yourselves.
Do what it says."

JAMES 1:22 (NIV)

STORY

Michaela loved reading devotionals and journaling about her faith.

But one day her friend said, "You talk about Jesus a lot — do you ever do what He says?"

At first, it stung. Then it sank in.

Faith wasn't meant to stay on a page — it was meant to move.

She started small — forgiving faster, helping quietly, listening more.

And her faith came alive.

Insight

Faith without action is just theory.

God's Word is powerful, but only when lived out.

You don't have to be loud — just consistent.
Real faith shows up in how you treat people every day.

"Faith grows strongest when your hands and heart work together."

Action Step

Do one thing today that puts your faith into action —
help, forgive, serve, or encourage.

Prayer

God, help me live what I believe.

Let my faith move from words to action. Amen.

Journal Prompt

What's one area of your life where your actions could
better reflect your faith?

God Still Speaks

"My sheep listen to my voice;
I know them, and they follow me."

JOHN 10:27 (NIV)

STORY

Chloe often wondered, *How do people "hear" God?*

She'd never heard a booming voice or seen a sign.

But one day while reading her Bible, a verse seemed to stand out like it was written just for her.

Later, during a walk, a peaceful thought crossed her mind that felt different — clearer, kinder.

That's when she realised: maybe God's voice wasn't loud, but it was real.

INSIGHT

God still speaks — through His Word, through peace in your heart, through wise people, through that quiet nudge inside.

You don't have to chase a dramatic moment. Just slow down and listen.

The more time you spend with Him, the easier it becomes to recognise His voice.

> *"God's voice isn't always loud — sometimes it's a whisper that calms your heart."*

ACTION STEP

Take 10 minutes in silence today — no music, no phone — and ask God to speak to your heart.

PRAYER

Lord, help me to recognise Your voice among all the noise.

Teach me to listen with peace and respond with faith. Amen.

JOURNAL PROMPT

When was the last time you felt like God was speaking to you — through Scripture, a thought, or a person?

Purpose in Pain

"And we know that in all things God works for the good of those who love him."

ROMANS 8:28 (NIV)

STORY

After losing her grandmother, Leah felt numb.

Everyone told her "time heals," but it didn't feel true.

Months later, she shared her story at youth group, and a girl came up in tears — she'd lost someone too.

In that moment, Leah realised her pain wasn't wasted. God was using it to help someone else heal.

INSIGHT

Pain doesn't mean God has left you.

He can turn your hardest moments into something beautiful — not by erasing them, but by using them.

When you give Him your broken pieces, He builds something stronger.

"Your story can bring healing to someone else's pain."

ACTION STEP

Reach out to someone who's struggling. You don't need the right words — just be there.

PRAYER

God, help me trust You with my pain.

Use my story to bring hope to someone else. Amen.

JOURNAL PROMPT

What's one painful thing God might be using to shape your strength or compassion?

Stay Real

*"People look at the outward appearance,
but the Lord looks at the heart."*

1 SAMUEL 16:7 (NIV)

STORY

Jordan always tried to impress people — new clothes, perfect selfies, pretending he was fine even when he wasn't.

But it was exhausting.

At a youth weekend, he heard, "God loves the real you — not the edited version."

For the first time, he dropped the act and prayed honestly.

It was scary, but freeing.

INSIGHT

God isn't looking for perfect; He's looking for honest.

You don't need to fake faith or hide your flaws.

He already knows your heart — and loves you anyway.

When you're real with God, He can do something real in you.

"Authenticity invites God's power where pretending shuts it out."

ACTION STEP

Talk to God today about something you've been hiding — no filters, just honesty.

PRAYER

Lord, thank You that I don't have to pretend with You. Help me live real and honest before You and others. Amen.

JOURNAL PROMPT

What's something you've been pretending is fine when it's not?

What would it look like to be honest about it?

Let Go and Let God

*"Trust in the Lord
with all your heart and lean not
on your own understanding."*

PROVERBS 3:5 (NIV)

STORY

Sam liked to plan everything — every detail, every outcome.

When things didn't go as expected, he got anxious.

But after a series of disappointments, he finally prayed, "God, I can't control this — You can."

It wasn't instant relief, but for the first time, he felt peace.

Letting go wasn't giving up — it was giving it to God.

INSIGHT

Sometimes faith means loosening your grip.

God sees the full picture when you only see one corner.

Letting go isn't losing control — it's trusting the One who's always been in control.

> *"The hands that made the world can handle your world too."*

ACTION STEP

Think of one thing stressing you out. Tell God, "I give this to You," and choose to trust Him with it.

PRAYER

God, I don't have to control everything — You do.

Help me to trust You with what I can't change.
Amen.

JOURNAL PROMPT

What's one situation you're struggling to surrender?

What might change if you trusted God with it?

Hope Wins

*"May the God of hope fill you with all
joy and peace as you trust in him."*

ROMANS 15:13 (NIV)

STORY

After a rough start to the year, Ella felt drained.

Nothing seemed to go right — friendships, grades,
even faith.

One morning, she wrote in her journal, "I just need
a reason to hope."

Later that day, a message popped up on her phone:
"Keep trusting. God's not finished."

Tears filled her eyes — not because her problems
disappeared, but because hope came back.

INSIGHT

Hope doesn't mean ignoring pain; it means believing it won't have the final say.

God's not finished with your story — and His ending is always good.

Hold on. The light is still coming.

> *"Hope is choosing to believe that God's best is still ahead."*

ACTION STEP

Encourage someone today with a message of hope — remind them that God's not done.

PRAYER

God of hope, fill me with joy and peace as I trust You.

Help me to keep believing, even when life feels hard. Amen.

JOURNAL PROMPT

Where do you need hope most right now?

What promise from God can you hold on to this week?

Identity Ignited

THEME RECAP

This month revealed who you are in Christ —
chosen, loved, seen, and set apart. You've learned
that identity isn't earned; it's discovered in God's
truth.

REFLECT

1. Which devotional spoke most deeply to your
   sense of identity?

2. How has your view of yourself changed since
   the start of the month?

3. What lie about yourself has God's truth helped
   you replace?

PRAY

Father, thank You for calling me Yours. Help me live from a place of confidence in who You've made me to be. Let my life reflect Your love and light. Amen.

ACTION

Write a short "Identity Declaration" — a few sentences beginning with "I am…" (e.g., I am chosen, forgiven, and loved. I am not an accident; I am part of God's plan.) Keep it in your journal or phone wallpaper as a reminder.

February

FAITH IN MOTION

Step Out of the Boat

*"Then Peter got down out
of the boat, walked on the water
and came toward Jesus."*

MATTHEW 14:29 (NIV)

STORY

Liam liked comfort zones.

He loved routines and didn't like change.

But when he felt God nudging him to join the worship team, he panicked — what if he failed?

One night, he read the story of Peter walking on water and realised: Peter only did the impossible *after* he stepped out.

So Liam said yes. It wasn't perfect, but it was faith in motion.

INSIGHT

Faith doesn't grow in comfort zones — it grows when you trust God enough to step out.

Fear says, "Stay safe." Faith says, "Move forward."

You'll never know what God can do until you take the first step.

> *"God can't steer a boat that*
> *never leaves the shore."*

ACTION STEP

Say yes to one thing God's been nudging you to do — even if it scares you.

PRAYER

Lord, help me to trust You enough to step out of my comfort zone.

I want to walk by faith, not fear. Amen.

JOURNAL PROMPT

What's one "boat" you need to step out of — an excuse, a fear, or a comfort zone?

Faith That Obeys

*"Blessed rather are those who
hear the word of God and obey it."*

LUKE 11:28 (NIV)

STORY

Nina loved hearing about faith, but obeying God?
That was harder.

When she felt God prompting her to apologise to
someone she'd hurt, she argued with herself all day.

Eventually, she swallowed her pride and sent a
message.

The moment she did, peace flooded her heart.
Obedience brought freedom.

INSIGHT

Faith isn't just believing — it's doing.

Obedience might cost your comfort, but it always brings blessing.

Every time you obey, you show God that you trust His way more than your own.

> ## *"Faith grows strongest when obedience feels hardest."*

ACTION STEP

Ask God if there's one thing He's asked you to do that you've been delaying. Then do it today.

PRAYER

God, give me courage to obey even when it's uncomfortable.

Help me trust that Your way is always best. Amen.

JOURNAL PROMPT

When was a time obedience felt hard but ended up being worth it?

3 FEBRUARY

Small Faith, Big God

*"Faith as small as a mustard
seed can move mountains."*

MATTHEW 17:20 (NIV)

STORY

Emma didn't think her prayers mattered much.

She'd whisper small ones — "God, help me today"
— but didn't expect big results.

Then her mum got better from an illness they'd
been praying about for weeks.

It reminded Emma that even small prayers, said
with sincere faith, reach a big God.

Insight

It's not the size of your faith that matters — it's the size of your God.

Even a tiny bit of trust can open the door for something huge.

God never ignores a heart that dares to believe.

> *"Small faith is still real faith*
> *— and that's enough."*

Action Step

Pray a "mustard seed" prayer today — something small but honest.

Prayer

God, thank You that even my little faith matters to You.

Help me to keep trusting You in the small things. Amen.

Journal Prompt

What's one small area of your life where you can start trusting God more?

Faith Over Fear (Again)

"When I am afraid,
I put my trust in you."

PSALM 56:3 (NIV)

STORY

Zoe struggled with anxiety about school presentations.

Her hands shook, and her heart raced every time she had to speak.

But before her last one, she whispered Psalm 56:3: "When I am afraid, I put my trust in You."

She still felt nervous, but the fear didn't control her — faith did.

INSIGHT

Faith doesn't mean fear disappears; it means fear doesn't win.

You can feel afraid and still trust God.

Courage isn't the absence of fear — it's moving forward in spite of it.

"Faith doesn't erase fear — it outlasts it."

ACTION STEP

Whenever fear hits today, say Psalm 56:3 out loud.

PRAYER

Lord, when fear shows up, help me remember You're bigger.

Let my trust be stronger than my worry. Amen.

JOURNAL PROMPT

What fear tries to hold you back most often?

How could faith respond instead?

Keep Going

*"Let us run with perseverance
the race marked out for us."*

HEBREWS 12:1 (NIV)

STORY

Darius started the year strong — praying, journaling, staying consistent.

But by February, he was tired.

One morning, his youth leader texted, "Don't quit. Faith isn't about speed — it's about consistency."

So he didn't. He prayed again that night — not perfectly, but faithfully.

Insight

Faith isn't a sprint; it's a marathon.

You don't have to be the fastest — just keep moving.

Even on slow days, you're still growing when you don't give up.

> ## *"Faith doesn't need perfection*
> *—just persistence."*

Action Step

Do one small thing today to strengthen your faith — pray, read a verse, or encourage someone.

Prayer

Lord, give me strength to keep going when I feel tired or distracted.

Thank You that You never give up on me. Amen.

Journal Prompt

What keeps you from being consistent in your faith?

What can help you stay steady?

Walk the Talk

*"Faith by itself, if it is not accompanied
by action, is dead."*

JAMES 2:17 (NIV)

STORY

Noah loved youth group. He sang loud, posted
Bible verses, and prayed before meals.

But at school, it was different — jokes went too far,
gossip spread, and he joined in.

One day, a friend said quietly, "You don't seem like
the
same person you are at church."

It stung — but it opened his eyes. Faith wasn't just
for Sundays; it was for every day.

INSIGHT

Faith is more than words — it's lifestyle.

People should be able to see your faith before you even talk about it.

When your actions match your beliefs, you show the world what God's love looks like in real life.

> *"Let your actions prove*
> *what your words say."*

ACTION STEP

Ask yourself before you speak or act today: "Does this show what I believe?"

PRAYER

Lord, help me live out my faith consistently.
I want people to see You through the way I act.
Amen.

JOURNAL PROMPT

Where do you find it hardest to live your faith out loud?

Faith That Serves

"Serve one another humbly in love."

GALATIANS 5:13 (NIV)

STORY

Mila didn't think serving was for her — she wasn't loud, talented, or "leader material."

But when her church needed help setting up chairs for an event, she volunteered anyway.

No spotlight. No applause. Just quiet faithfulness.

At the end, her youth leader said, "You served like Jesus today."

That was all she needed to hear.

INSIGHT

Faith that works is faith that serves.

You don't need a stage to make an impact — just a willing heart.

Jesus showed that real greatness comes through humility.

> *"Faith looks most like Jesus when*
> *it serves without needing credit."*

ACTION STEP

Do one small act of service today — help at home, encourage someone, or volunteer.

PRAYER

Jesus, teach me to serve like You — with humility, love, and joy. Amen.

JOURNAL PROMPT

How could serving others help your faith grow stronger?

Faith That Forgives

"Forgive as the Lord forgave you."
COLOSSIANS 3:13 (NIV)

STORY

Eli couldn't forgive his friend who betrayed him.

Every time he saw him, the anger came back.

Then his pastor said, "Forgiveness isn't saying what they did was okay — it's saying you're done carrying it."

Eli prayed, "God, help me let go."

It took time, but slowly the bitterness lost its grip.

INSIGHT

Forgiveness isn't weakness — it's freedom.

When you forgive, you're not saying the hurt didn't matter; you're saying God *matters more*.

Unforgiveness chains your heart, but grace sets it free.

> *"You can't move forward if you're still chained to yesterday."*

ACTION STEP

Think of someone you need to forgive — even if it's yourself. Pray for strength to release them.

PRAYER

God, thank You for forgiving me.
Help me forgive others like You do — fully and freely.
Amen.

JOURNAL PROMPT

Who do you need to forgive?

What might happen if you finally did?

Faith That Trusts

"Trust in the Lord with all your heart and lean not on your own understanding."

PROVERBS 3:5 (NIV)

STORY

Sophie liked to figure everything out.

When things didn't make sense, she worried and overthought.

Then she read Proverbs 3:5 and realised — maybe she didn't need to understand everything, just trust the One who does.

That night, she prayed, "God, I don't get it, but I'll trust You anyway."

Peace followed.

INSIGHT

Trust doesn't mean you stop thinking; it means you stop controlling.

Faith works best when you put it in God's hands and let go of your grip.

When you trust Him, confusion turns into calm.

*"Faith starts where
your understanding ends."*

ACTION STEP

Write down one thing you're trying to control.
Pray and give it to God.

PRAYER

Lord, teach me to trust You with all my heart — even when I don't understand. Amen.

JOURNAL PROMPT

Where are you leaning on your own understanding instead of God's wisdom?

Faith That Loves

"Let all that you do be done in love."

1 CORINTHIANS 16:14 (ESV)

STORY

Isaac found it easy to love people who were kind — but not so much the rude ones.

When a classmate mocked him for being Christian, he wanted to snap back.

Then he remembered Jesus' words about loving enemies.

He took a breath, said nothing cruel, and prayed for the boy later that night.

It wasn't easy — but it was love in action.

INSIGHT

Faith without love is noise.

Real faith loves people who are hard to love, because that's what Jesus did.

Love isn't weakness — it's the strongest kind of courage.

> ## *"The strongest people love even when it's hardest."*

ACTION STEP

Show love to someone difficult today — through kindness, patience, or prayer.

PRAYER

God, help me to love like You — not just in words, but in how I live. Amen.

JOURNAL PROMPT

Who's one person that's hard to love right now?

How can you show them God's love this week?

When Faith Feels Hard

"Consider it pure joy, my brothers and sisters, whenever you face trials of many kinds."

JAMES 1:2 (NIV)

STORY

Hannah didn't understand why bad things kept happening.

She prayed, stayed kind, and tried to do right — yet her parents argued, her grades slipped, and life just felt heavy.

One night, she told God, "I don't get this."

Later, she read James 1:2 and thought, *Joy? In this?*

Then she realised — joy wasn't pretending things were okay. It was trusting God was working through them.

INSIGHT

Faith isn't proved when everything's perfect — it's proved when everything hurts.

God never wastes pain; He uses it to grow strength, empathy, and trust in your heart.

You don't have to enjoy the trial — but you can trust the outcome.

"Tough times don't break real faith; they build it."

ACTION STEP

Think of one hard thing you're facing. Ask God to help you see how He might use it for good.

PRAYER

God, help me to keep trusting You even when faith feels hard.

Remind me that every test can grow my strength. Amen.

JOURNAL PROMPT

What's one lesson you've learned through something difficult?

Tempted but Not Trapped

"God is faithful; he will not let you be tempted beyond what you can bear."

1 CORINTHIANS 10:13 (NIV)

STORY

Theo wanted to do the right thing, but temptation was real — to cheat, to lie, to fit in.

He thought, *Everyone else does it*, but guilt always followed.

Then he read 1 Corinthians 10:13 and realised temptation wasn't unbeatable — there was always a way out.

Next time it came, he prayed for strength, walked away, and found peace instead of regret.

Insight

Everyone faces temptation — even Jesus did.

Temptation isn't sin; giving in is.

God always provides a way out — sometimes through courage, other times through escape.

You're never too weak to say "no" when His Spirit lives in you.

> *"Temptation tests your faith,*
> *but it doesn't have to define it."*

Action Step

When you face temptation today, pause and pray: "Lord, show me the way out."

Prayer

Lord, help me to recognise temptation early and choose Your way over my way. Amen.

Journal Prompt

What's one temptation you face often?

What "way out" could you take next time?

Faith vs. Fear

*"For God has not given us a spirit of fear,
but of power, love and self-control."*

2 TIMOTHY 1:7 (NIV)

STORY

Eli dreaded public speaking.

When his teacher announced he'd been chosen to represent the class, panic hit.

He almost said no — until he remembered a verse from youth group: *"God hasn't given me a spirit of fear."*

He prayed, took a deep breath, and did it.

His hands shook, but he made it through — and smiled.

Insight

Fear whispers, "You can't."

Faith replies, "With God, I can."

Courage doesn't mean you don't feel scared; it means fear doesn't control your decisions.

The Spirit inside you is stronger than the fear outside you.

> *"Fear may visit, but it doesn't get to move in."*

Action Step

Do one thing this week that fear has tried to stop you from doing.

Prayer

God, fill me with courage and peace.

Remind me that fear isn't from You — and I don't have to live by it. Amen.

Journal Prompt

Where has fear held you back?

What's one small step of courage you could take?

Faithful, Not Perfect

*"My grace is sufficient for you, for
my power is made perfect in weakness."*

2 CORINTHIANS 12:9 (NIV)

STORY

Lara compared herself to everyone.

Other Christians seemed stronger, more consistent,
more spiritual.

She often thought, *Why can't I be like them?*

Then she read Paul's words about weakness and
realised God wasn't waiting for her to be perfect —
just faithful.

Her flaws became the very places His strength
showed up.

INSIGHT

God's not looking for perfection — He's looking for persistence.

He shines through your weakness, not your performance.

When you bring Him your flaws, He fills them with His grace.

> *"You don't need to be flawless
> — just faithful."*

ACTION STEP

Write down one area of weakness and thank God that His strength covers it.

PRAYER

Lord, thank You that Your grace is enough.
Use my weakness to show Your power.
Amen.

JOURNAL PROMPT

Where do you feel weak right now? How might God be showing His strength through it?

Never Alone in the Fire

"When you walk through the fire, you will not be burned."

ISAIAH 43:2 (NIV)

STORY

Tomi felt like everything was falling apart — school stress, arguments at home, and feeling distant from friends.

He prayed, "God, where are You?"

Later, during worship, he felt a quiet reminder: *I'm right here.*

The situation didn't change overnight, but Tomi did.

He stopped trying to escape the fire — and started walking through it with God beside him.

INSIGHT

God never promised to keep you out of every fire, but He did promise to be with you in it.

Your strength doesn't come from escaping pain — it comes from His presence inside it.

You might feel the heat, but you won't be consumed.

> *"God doesn't always put out the fire — sometimes He joins you in it."*

ACTION STEP

If life feels heavy, take a moment to thank God that you're not facing it alone.

PRAYER

Lord, thank You for staying with me through every storm and fire.

Help me to feel Your presence when life gets tough. Amen.

JOURNAL PROMPT

What's one "fire" you're walking through?

Where can you see signs that God's been with you?

The Battle Belongs to God

*"The Lord will fight for you;
you need only to be still."*

EXODUS 14:14 (NIV)

STORY

Kenny hated conflict. When his friendship group fell apart, he tried to fix it all himself — sending texts, apologising, stressing over every detail.

But nothing worked.

Then during his quiet time, he read Exodus 14:14. It felt like God whispering, *"Stop fighting battles that aren't yours."*

So he did. He prayed instead of panicking — and peace came before the solution did.

Insight

You're not meant to fight every battle alone.

Some situations require silence, prayer, and trust —
not strategy.

When you let God take over, you'll find peace that striving
can't bring.

> *"Sometimes faith means*
> *putting the sword down*
> *and letting God fight."*

Action Step

If you're in a conflict or challenge, pause and pray:
"God, this battle is Yours."

Prayer

Lord, remind me that You fight for me.
Help me to stay calm and trust Your plan.
Amen.

Journal Prompt

What's one "battle" you've been trying to control?

How could you give it back to God today?

Victory in Weakness

"In all these things we are
more than conquerors through
him who loved us."

ROMANS 8:37 (NIV)

STORY

Tiana always felt like she was losing — losing focus, losing confidence, losing hope.

At youth group, her leader read Romans 8:37 and said, "You're not fighting *for* victory — you're fighting *from* it."

That sentence stayed with her.

She wasn't a failure trying to win; she was a conqueror learning to stand.

Insight

Your victory isn't based on your strength — it's rooted in God's love.

Even when you fall, that love keeps you standing.

You may feel weak, but in Jesus, you're already on the winning side.

> *"You're not fighting for victory*
> *— you're standing in it."*

Action Step

When you feel defeated today, say out loud: "I'm more than a conqueror in Christ."

Prayer

God, thank You that victory is already mine in You. Help me to walk in that truth with confidence. Amen.

Journal Prompt

Where have you been feeling defeated lately?

What truth reminds you that God's already won?

Fight with Faith

"Fight the good fight of the faith."
1 TIMOTHY 6:12 (NIV)

STORY

Jerome was tired — tired of trying, tired of pressure, tired of pretending.

One morning, his mum said, "Don't give up — fight with faith."

He didn't fully get it until he prayed instead of complaining.

Something changed inside him — not his situation, but his strength.

INSIGHT

The fight of faith isn't against people — it's against doubt, fear, and discouragement.

Every prayer, every act of obedience, every moment you don't quit — that's faith fighting.

You don't need fists to win spiritual battles; you need faith that won't back down.

"Faith doesn't give up
— it gets up."

ACTION STEP

If you feel tired, pray this simple line: "God, help me fight with faith today."

PRAYER

Lord, when I feel weak, remind me that You're my strength. Help me to keep fighting with faith, not frustration. Amen.

JOURNAL PROMPT

What's one battle you need to face with faith instead of fear?

Faith That Endures

*"Let perseverance finish its work so
that you may be mature and complete."*

JAMES 1:4 (NIV)

STORY

Nadine started strong in her faith — daily devotions, prayer, worship.

But after a while, she felt dry. Nothing exciting was happening.

Then her youth leader said, "Faith isn't about constant fireworks; it's about steady flames."

That line stuck.

She kept showing up — and eventually, her passion reignited.

INSIGHT

Faith isn't built in the moments that feel amazing; it's built in the moments you keep going when nothing feels special.

Endurance doesn't look exciting, but it's how real strength grows.

> *"Faith that lasts is faith that stays*
> *— even when it's quiet."*

ACTION STEP

Stay consistent today in one small faith habit — prayer, gratitude, or kindness.

PRAYER

God, help me stay faithful even when I don't feel inspired. Teach me that lasting faith is built through endurance. Amen.

JOURNAL PROMPT

Where are you tempted to give up?

How could you stay steady there?

Faith Over Feelings (Part 2)

"The righteous will live by faith."

ROMANS 1:17 (NIV)

STORY

Callum often said, "I don't feel close to God anymore."
His youth pastor replied, "That's why we live by faith, not feelings."

At first, it sounded too simple — but it made sense. Faith isn't about a constant emotional high; it's about choosing trust daily.

So Callum kept praying, even on dry days — and slowly, joy returned.

Insight

Faith isn't fragile — it's steady.

Feelings shift, but truth doesn't.

Even when emotions fade, obedience keeps you connected.

God is present, even when He feels silent.

> *"Faith walks steady*
> *when feelings walk away."*

Action Step

When you don't feel close to God, do one thing that keeps you walking by faith — pray, read, or worship anyway.

Prayer

Lord, help me follow You faithfully, not just emotionally. Even when I don't feel it, I'll keep trusting You. Amen.

Journal Prompt

When do your feelings make faith hard?

What helps you keep trusting anyway?

Better Together

"Two are better than one, because they have a good return for their labour."

ECCLESIASTES 4:9 (NIV)

STORY

Leah tried doing faith alone.

She skipped youth group, avoided church, and told herself she could handle things solo.

But when she started to struggle, the silence was deafening.

One Sunday she finally went back — hesitant but hungry — and her friends welcomed her with open arms.

That day she realised: she didn't need to have it all together to belong.

INSIGHT

You were never meant to walk alone.

Faith grows best in community — where people remind you who you are when you forget.

Even when you want to isolate, connection is where healing happens.

"Faith is personal but never meant to be private."

ACTION STEP

Reach out to one person in your church or youth group today — check in, encourage, or just connect.

PRAYER

Lord, thank You for putting people in my life who lift me up.

Help me to value community and stay connected. Amen.

JOURNAL PROMPT

Who encourages your faith the most — and how could you thank them this week?

Real Friends, Real Faith

"A friend loves at all times."

PROVERBS 17:17 (NIV)

STORY

Ethan realised not all friendships last forever.

Some people drifted when things got tough, but others stayed and prayed.

One friend texted him every morning for a week: "Don't give up."

That small act helped Ethan see the difference between a friend who just hangs out — and one who holds you up.

INSIGHT

Good friends are a gift from God — but godly friends are a lifeline.

Real friends tell you the truth, cheer you on, and stay even when things get messy.

Choose friends who feed your faith, not your fear.

> *"The right friends don't pull you away from God — they pull you closer."*

ACTION STEP

Send a message to a friend who's helped your faith. Let them know they matter.

PRAYER

God, thank You for real friends who make faith easier. Help me be that kind of friend to someone else. Amen.

JOURNAL PROMPT

What qualities make a true friend in your eyes?

How could you be one this week?

Encourage Someone Today

"Therefore encourage one another and build each other up."

1 THESSALONIANS 5:11 (NIV)

STORY

Maya noticed her classmate looked down all week.

She wanted to help but didn't know what to say.

Finally, she left a small note on their desk: "You're doing better than you think."

The next day, that classmate smiled for the first time in days.

It reminded Maya that encouragement doesn't need to be loud — just genuine.

Insight

Encouragement is one of the most powerful gifts you can give.

You never know what someone's fighting silently — your words might be what keeps them going.

Faith that works always builds others up.

> *"You might not fix someone's day, but you can light it up."*

Action Step

Say or write one genuine compliment or encouragement to someone today.

Prayer

Lord, make me someone who lifts others up with my words. Use me to spread kindness that points to You. Amen.

Journal Prompt

Who around you could use encouragement right now?

How could you offer it?

Faith That Unites

"Make every effort to keep the unity
of the Spirit through the bond of peace."

EPHESIANS 4:3 (NIV)

STORY

Youth group was divided — cliques, gossip, and cold shoulders.

During one meeting, their leader said, "If we can't love each other here, how will we love the world out there?"

The words stung but sparked change.

The next week, a few teens apologised, prayed together, and something shifted.

They didn't all become best friends — but they became family again.

INSIGHT

Unity doesn't mean everyone's the same — it means everyone's focused on the same purpose: Jesus.

When love leads, division fades.

A united faith family becomes unstoppable.

> *"Unity isn't about being identical — it's about being in sync with God's heart."*

ACTION STEP

If there's tension in your group or friendship, take the first step toward peace.

PRAYER

God, help me to be a peacemaker in my circle.
Let love, not pride, guide my actions. Amen.

JOURNAL PROMPT

Where could you help bring peace instead of adding to conflict?

We're All Parts of the Body

*"Now you are the body of Christ,
and each one of you is a part of it."*

1 CORINTHIANS 12:27 (NIV)

STORY

During a youth event, the leader gave everyone puzzle pieces.

At first, no one saw the point. But when they fit them together, it formed a cross.

"Every piece matters," she said. "So does every person."

That day, Jayden realised something: even if he didn't sing, preach, or lead, he still had a purpose.

INSIGHT

You're not a spare part — you're a vital piece of what God's building.

When everyone plays their part, the Church shines brighter.

Faith in motion means using your gifts for something bigger than yourself.

> *"You don't have to do everything —*
> *just the thing God made you for."*

ACTION STEP

Ask God to show you one way to serve or contribute in your church this week.

PRAYER

Lord, thank You that I'm part of Your body.
Show me how to use my gifts to build Your Kingdom.
Amen.

JOURNAL PROMPT

What's one gift, skill, or passion you have that you could offer to serve God?

Shine Anyway

"You are the light of the world.
A city on a hill cannot be hidden."

MATTHEW 5:14 (NIV)

STORY

Zara used to stay quiet about her faith.

She didn't want to seem "too religious" or get teased.

But after a friend went through a hard time, Zara felt God nudge her to pray for her — right there in school.

Her voice shook, but she did it.

Later, her friend said, "I really needed that."

That moment changed everything.

Insight

Your faith isn't meant to hide; it's meant to shine.

People need light — and you carry it.

Even small acts of courage can spark hope in someone's darkness.

"Don't dim your light because someone else prefers the dark."

Action Step

Do one thing today that lets your light shine — pray, help, speak up, or share hope.

Prayer

Jesus, help me shine Your light with courage and love. Let my life draw others closer to You. Amen.

Journal Prompt

Where can you shine brighter — at school, home, or online?

Faith That Shares

*"Go into all the world and preach
the gospel to all creation."*

MARK 16:15 (NIV)

STORY

Tomi loved God but felt awkward sharing his faith.

He thought evangelism was only for confident people with microphones.

Then one day, his friend asked, "Why do you always seem calm, even when things go wrong?"

Tomi just smiled and said, "Because I know God's got me."

That simple answer opened a whole conversation about Jesus.

Insight

You don't need a stage to share your faith — just a story and a heart.

Your kindness, peace, and love might be the sermon someone needs to hear.

Faith that's real naturally overflows into others' lives.

"You don't have to know all the answers — just share the difference Jesus made in you."

Action Step

Pray for one person who doesn't know God yet. Ask Him to show you a way to share His love with them.

Prayer

Lord, give me courage to share my faith with love, not pressure.

Let my life point people to You. Amen.

Journal Prompt

Who in your life needs to hear about God's love?

How could you start the conversation naturally?

Faith That Gives

*"It is more blessed to give
than to receive."*

ACTS 20:35 (NIV)

STORY

Amira saved for months to buy new trainers.

But when she heard about a mission trip fundraiser, she felt God whisper, *"Give it."*

It was hard — but she did.

Later, she found out her donation helped send supplies to a school overseas.

The joy she felt lasted longer than any new shoes could.

Insight

Generosity isn't about how much you have; it's about how much you're willing to give.

Faith that gives freely reflects a heart that trusts God to provide.

When you bless others, you become part of God's miracle.

"You don't lose by giving — you grow."

Action Step

Give something today — time, encouragement, money, or help — with no expectation in return.

Prayer

Lord, make me generous with what I have.
Teach me to give with joy and faith. Amen.

Journal Prompt

What's one way you could practise generosity this week?

Live Bold

"The righteous are as bold as a lion."

PROVERBS 28:1 (NIV)

STORY

Jonah used to stay quiet when people made fun of Christians.

He didn't want to argue or stand out.

But after reading Proverbs 28:1, he prayed for boldness.

A few days later, a classmate mocked his faith — and Jonah simply replied, "I believe in Jesus because He changed my life."

The room went silent. Not because he was loud, but because he was confident.

Insight

Bold faith doesn't mean being loud — it means being unashamed.

When you stand firm, others notice.

You don't have to defend God — just represent Him with courage and grace.

> *"Be bold, not to impress*
> *— but to express the God*
> *who lives in you."*

Action Step

Ask God for boldness to be real about your faith wherever you go.

Prayer

Lord, give me courage to stand strong and live boldly for You. Let my life be a fearless reflection of Your love. Amen.

Journal Prompt

Where do you need more boldness — in words, actions, or faith?

Faith in Motion

THEME RECAP

This month taught you that faith is active — it walks, serves, forgives, and endures. You've learned that trusting God means acting on His Word, even when it's hard.

REFLECT

1. What step of obedience or courage have you taken this month?

2. Where did you see God's faithfulness as you moved in faith?

3. What habit or relationship helped your faith grow stronger?

PRAY

Lord, thank You for showing me that faith isn't a feeling — it's a daily choice. Help me to keep walking with You in trust and boldness. Amen.

ACTION

Choose one way to live out your faith this week — share your story, serve someone quietly, or forgive where it's overdue.

March

LIVING SET APART

Stay Rooted

"Let your roots grow down into him,
and let your lives be built on him."

COLOSSIANS 2:7 (NLT)

STORY

When the storm hit last winter, a big tree outside the youth hall snapped in half.

But another tree beside it stood tall. Its roots ran deep.

Later, their youth leader said, "That's what faith should look like."

It clicked for Jamal — roots aren't seen, but they're what keep you standing when everything shakes.

Insight

Faith isn't just about moments of passion; it's about deep roots in God's truth.

When you stay rooted — in prayer, Scripture, and community — you don't fall when life storms hit.

> *"The deeper your roots,*
> *the stronger your stand."*

Action Step

Spend 10 minutes reading one chapter from the Gospels today. Ask God to grow your roots deeper in Him.

Prayer

Lord, help me grow roots that hold fast in every season. Let my faith be steady, not shallow. Amen.

Journal Prompt

What helps your faith feel "rooted" instead of shaky?

Don't Rush the Process

"There is a time for everything."

ECCLESIASTES 3:1 (NIV)

STORY

Amara wanted quick results — quick answers, quick growth, quick blessings.

When she didn't see progress, she assumed something was wrong.

But while baking one day, she realised — even cake takes time. You can't rush it without ruining it.

Faith is the same: some things need time to rise.

INSIGHT

Spiritual growth takes time.

God's not slow — He's strategic.

Every delay is part of His design to strengthen your patience and deepen your trust.

> *"Faith doesn't grow in a hurry*
> *— it grows in the waiting."*

ACTION STEP

Be patient with one area of your life that feels slow.
Thank God for working, even when you can't see it.

PRAYER

Lord, teach me to trust Your timing more than my own.
Help me grow at Your pace, not mine. Amen.

JOURNAL PROMPT

What's something you've been rushing? How might God be using this season to grow you?

Stay Connected

"Remain in me,
as I also remain in you."

JOHN 15:4 (NIV)

STORY

Ava's phone battery was dying every few hours.

She realised she kept forgetting to charge it overnight.

That's when it hit her — her faith felt the same.

She hadn't been spending time with God, and her "spiritual battery" was running low.

INSIGHT

You can't live disconnected and expect to stay strong.

Faith fades without daily connection.

Jesus doesn't ask for perfection — just presence.

Stay plugged into Him, and you'll always find strength.

"Faith needs recharging — stay plugged into the Source."

ACTION STEP

Spend a few minutes today praying or journaling — reconnect intentionally.

PRAYER

Jesus, help me stay connected to You daily.
Remind me that I'm strongest when I remain in You.
Amen.

JOURNAL PROMPT

What helps you feel closest to God — and what tends to disconnect you?

Faith That Feeds on Truth

"Man shall not live on bread alone, but on every word that comes from the mouth of God."

MATTHEW 4:4 (NIV)

STORY

Caleb scrolled endlessly through social media, feeding his mind with everything but truth.

Then one day he realised — he'd spent more time online than in God's Word.

So he started reading one verse each morning before checking his phone.

It didn't change everything overnight, but it changed *him*.

Insight

Your mind needs feeding — and what you feed it with shapes your life.

God's Word nourishes faith like food nourishes your body. When you stay full of truth, lies lose their power.

> *"What you feed grows*
> *— so feed your faith."*

Action Step

Read one Psalm or one verse before opening social media today. Let God's Word go first.

Prayer

Lord, fill my mind with Your truth.
Help me crave Your Word more than the world's noise.
Amen.

Journal Prompt

What kind of "spiritual diet" are you on right now — and does it feed or drain your faith?

Faith That Prays

"Pray without ceasing."

1 THESSALONIANS 5:17 (NIV)

STORY

Riley used to think prayer had to be long and fancy.

Then one day she whispered, "God, I'm tired," and felt His peace wash over her.

That's when she realised — prayer isn't about perfect words; it's about real ones.

INSIGHT

Prayer keeps faith alive.

It's not a task; it's a relationship.

The more you talk to God — in your own way, in every moment — the more you recognise His voice in your life.

> ### "Prayer isn't a ritual — it's a heartbeat."

ACTION STEP

Talk to God throughout your day — while walking, studying, or resting. Keep the conversation open.

PRAYER

Lord, teach me to pray with honesty, not just habit. Let talking to You become my first reaction, not my last resort. Amen.

JOURNAL PROMPT

When does prayer feel most real to you — and what helps you keep it consistent?

Stretch to Grow

*"Grow in the grace and knowledge
of our Lord and Saviour Jesus Christ."*

2 PETER 3:18 (NIV)

STORY

At football practice, Nate hated stretching.

It was uncomfortable — but skipping it made him sore later.

One day his coach said, "Growth and comfort don't mix."

That hit him spiritually too.

Maybe the reason his faith felt stuck was because he'd stopped letting God stretch him.

Insight

Growth doesn't happen in comfort zones.

When God stretches you — through challenges, patience, or change — He's expanding your capacity for faith.

Don't fight the stretch; it's shaping you.

> *"Growth begins*
> *where comfort ends."*

Action Step

Say yes to one challenge that makes you depend more on God than yourself.

Prayer

Lord, help me embrace growth even when it's uncomfortable.

Stretch my faith and strengthen my trust. Amen.

Journal Prompt

What "stretch" are you facing right now that might actually be helping you grow?

Stay Teachable

*"Instruct the wise and
they will be wiser still."*

PROVERBS 9:9 (NIV)

STORY

Jasmine thought she knew everything.

Whenever someone corrected her, she got defensive.

Then a mentor said, "You're smart — but teachable people go further."

That stung, but it stuck.

She realised humility wasn't weakness — it was the doorway to growth.

INSIGHT

Faith grows when you stay teachable.

God sends lessons through people, Scripture, and even mistakes.

Pride blocks learning; humility invites it.

Every day, there's something new God wants to show you.

> *"If you stop learning,*
> *you stop growing."*

ACTION STEP

Ask someone you respect what they've learned about faith recently — and really listen.

PRAYER

Lord, make my heart teachable.
Help me learn from others and grow wiser through
Your Word. Amen.

JOURNAL PROMPT

Who in your life challenges you to grow — and what have they taught you?

Faith That Listens

*"Speak, Lord,
for your servant is listening."*

1 SAMUEL 3:10 (NIV)

STORY

During youth retreat, the leader asked everyone to sit in silence for five minutes.

No phones. No music. Just quiet.

At first, Tessa was bored. But after a while, she felt peace — like God was whispering calm into her thoughts.

It reminded her that listening *is* part of prayer.

INSIGHT

Faith isn't just about talking to God — it's about listening too.

He speaks through His Word, through peace, and through that still, small voice in your heart.

Silence isn't empty when you fill it with His presence.

> ## *"You can't hear God's voice if you never stop talking."*

ACTION STEP

Take five minutes today to be still and simply say, "Speak, Lord — I'm listening."

PRAYER

Lord, help me recognise Your voice above all the noise. Teach me to listen with my heart, not just my ears. Amen.

JOURNAL PROMPT

When was the last time you sensed God speaking to you — and what did He say?

Faith That Disciplines Itself

*"Run in such a way
as to get the prize."*

1 CORINTHIANS 9:24 (NIV)

STORY

Eli loved starting new habits — but hated keeping them.

He'd read his Bible for three days, then forget for a week.

Then he joined a gym, and the trainer said, "You can't build strength without consistency."

He realised faith worked the same way — discipline builds strength.

INSIGHT

Faith doesn't grow by accident — it grows by discipline.

Prayer, Scripture, and kindness aren't random acts; they're daily choices.

Discipline turns belief into lifestyle.

> *"Faith grows through repetition, not perfection."*

ACTION STEP

Choose one habit to build this week — prayer, gratitude, or reading the Bible — and stick to it daily.

PRAYER

God, give me focus to build strong habits of faith.
Help me stay consistent, even when I don't feel like it.
Amen.

JOURNAL PROMPT

What's one spiritual habit you want to grow more consistent in — and what's stopping you?

Faith That Learns From Failure

*"Though the righteous fall seven times,
they rise again."*

PROVERBS 24:16 (NIV)

STORY

Mika messed up — again.

She promised she'd stop losing her temper, but she slipped.

She cried, thinking God must be tired of her.

Then she read Proverbs 24:16 and realised — God's grace doesn't run out.

Falling isn't failure; refusing to get up is.

Insight

Failure isn't the end — it's feedback.

God uses mistakes to build humility and resilience.

Every time you rise again, your faith grows stronger roots.

> *"Falling down isn't failing*
> *— staying down is."*

Action Step

Think of a recent mistake. Ask God what lesson
He's teaching you through it.

Prayer

Lord, thank You that Your grace lifts me when I fall.
Help me rise again, stronger than before.
Amen.

Journal Prompt

What's one area where you've fallen — and what has
God taught you through it?

When You Feel Like Giving Up

"Let us not become weary in doing good,
for at the proper time we will
reap a harvest if we do not give up."

GALATIANS 6:9 (NIV)

STORY

Nia felt like nothing was working — school, friendships, even her faith.

She prayed, but it felt like her prayers bounced off the ceiling.

One night, she said, "God, I can't keep doing this."

The next morning, her daily verse popped up: *"Don't give up."*

It felt small, but it was enough to get through the day.

INSIGHT

Even strong believers get tired.

But faith that lasts doesn't quit when it's hard — it leans in harder.

God is never absent in your exhaustion; He's whispering, *"Keep going — I'm still here."*

> ### *"When you're down to nothing, God's up to something."*

ACTION STEP

If you feel like quitting something good, pause and pray before you decide.

PRAYER

Lord, when I feel tired or discouraged, remind me You're still working.

Give me strength to keep going, even when it's tough. Amen.

JOURNAL PROMPT

What's one thing you're tempted to give up on — and what keeps you holding on?

Faith That Waits

*"Be still before the Lord
and wait patiently for him."*

PSALM 37:7 (NIV)

STORY

Tyler prayed for months for an answer about his future — nothing came.

He started doubting if God even cared.

But during a youth service, the speaker said, "If it's taking time, it's because God's preparing the blessing *and* the person."

That line hit deep.

Tyler realised waiting wasn't punishment — it was preparation.

INSIGHT

Waiting builds faith muscles you can't grow any other way.

God's timing is perfect — not just for the outcome, but for your heart.

He's never late; He's just aligning things beyond what you can see.

> *"Delay isn't denial*
> *— it's development."*

ACTION STEP

Instead of asking *"When, God?"* ask *"What are You teaching me in the wait?"*

PRAYER

God, help me to wait well — with patience, faith, and peace.

Teach me to trust Your timing fully. Amen.

JOURNAL PROMPT

How do you usually respond to waiting?

What could waiting be teaching you right now?

Faith That Hopes Again

*"We have this hope as an anchor
for the soul, firm and secure."*

HEBREWS 6:19 (NIV)

STORY

After a series of disappointments, Bella stopped expecting good things.

She smiled, but inside she'd lost hope.

Then a mentor gave her a bracelet that said *"Anchored."*

"Hope keeps you steady," she said. "Storms don't move anchors."

Bella realised hope wasn't wishful thinking — it was choosing to believe God still had good ahead.

INSIGHT

Hope isn't pretending everything's fine; it's believing God's promise stands even when life shakes.

It's the quiet strength that keeps your heart steady when you can't see the way forward.

> *"Hope is faith holding on through the night."*

ACTION STEP

Write one promise from God you're holding onto — and keep it where you'll see it daily.

PRAYER

Lord, when hope feels hard, anchor my heart in Your promises.

Help me believe again. Amen.

JOURNAL PROMPT

What's something you've stopped hoping for — and how can you start hoping again?

Faith That Overcomes Doubt

"I do believe;
help me overcome my unbelief!"

MARK 9:24 (NIV)

STORY

Jacob always wondered if his faith was "enough."

He compared himself to others who seemed more spiritual.

One day, during a youth talk, the leader said, "Faith isn't the absence of doubt — it's choosing to trust anyway."

That line set him free.

Doubt didn't disqualify him — it just meant he was human.

Insight

Doubt doesn't make you weak — it gives you a chance to grow deeper.

Bring your questions to God; He can handle them.

Real faith isn't pretending to have it all figured out — it's clinging to God when you don't.

> ### *"God's not afraid of your questions — He invites them."*

Action Step

Be honest with God about one question or doubt you've been hiding.

Prayer

God, thank You that You love me through my doubts. Help me to keep trusting even when I don't understand everything. Amen.

Journal Prompt

What's one question about faith you'd love to ask God — and what might His gentle answer be?

Faith That Endures the Storm

*"When the storms of life come,
the righteous stand firm."*

PROVERBS 10:25 (NLT)

STORY

Lola's family went through a tough season —
money
was tight, and stress was high.

She watched her mum pray every morning, even
through tears.

It amazed her that faith could survive a storm —
not because life was easy, but because God was real.

Years later, Lola prayed the same way.

INSIGHT

Storms don't mean God left — they often prove He's holding you closer.

When your world shakes, faith doesn't crumble; it clings.

You might bend, but you won't break when your roots are in Him.

> *"Faith doesn't stop the storm — it steadies you through it."*

ACTION STEP

If you're facing something tough, write down how you've seen God stay faithful before — and thank Him.

PRAYER

Lord, thank You for being my anchor in every storm. Help me stand firm, knowing You're holding me. Amen.

JOURNAL PROMPT

What's a "storm" you've been through — and how did God bring you through it?

Finish What You Started

"Being confident of this, that he who began a good work in you will carry it on to completion."

PHILIPPIANS 1:6 (NIV)

STORY

Amari started a new Bible plan every January — and usually quit by February.

This time, he decided to keep going, even when it got boring or hard.

Months later, he looked back and realised he'd finished something for the first time.

He smiled — because it wasn't about perfection, it was about persistence.

INSIGHT

God never starts something He doesn't plan to finish
— and neither should you.

Faith that lasts doesn't rely on motivation; it relies
on commitment.

Keep showing up — progress is built one small, steady
step at a time.

> *"God finishes what He starts*
> *— and so should you."*

ACTION STEP

Choose one thing — a goal, a habit, or a prayer — and
commit to finishing it this month.

PRAYER

Lord, help me stay focused and finish what You've
started in me.

Give me strength to stay faithful until the end.
Amen.

JOURNAL PROMPT

What's one thing you've started but not finished —
and what's stopping you from completing it?

Run Your Race

*"Let us run with perseverance
the race marked out for us."*

HEBREWS 12:1 (NIV)

STORY

During sports day, Malik started fast — then
slowed down when he saw others ahead.

But his coach yelled, "Run *your* race!"

He picked up speed and finished strong.

Later that week, during Bible study, he realised —
comparison had slowed more than his feet;
it had slowed his faith.

INSIGHT

You're not in competition with anyone.

God's plan for your life is unique — no one else can run it for you.

Focus on your lane, your pace, and your purpose.

> *"Faith runs best when*
> *you stop comparing tracks."*

ACTION STEP

Unfollow or mute anything on social media that triggers comparison. Refocus on your own journey.

PRAYER

God, help me to stay focused on my own race.
Teach me to celebrate others while staying faithful
to my lane. Amen.

JOURNAL PROMPT

Where are you tempted to compare yourself to others
— and how can you refocus on your race?

Keep the Fire Burning

"Never be lacking in zeal, but keep your spiritual fervour, serving the Lord."

ROMANS 12:11 (NIV)

STORY

During youth camp, everyone felt on fire for God — passionate, excited, unstoppable.

But a few weeks later, the spark faded.

Eve missed the feeling, until her youth leader said, "Fire doesn't keep itself burning — you have to feed it."

That night, she opened her Bible again — not for the feeling, but for the flame.

Insight

Faith isn't meant to burn out; it's meant to burn steady.

Keep feeding it with prayer, worship, and the Word.

When you feel dry, don't quit — refuel.

> ## "Spiritual fire doesn't fade
> — it just needs feeding."

Action Step

Do one thing today that reignites your faith — worship, journal, or pray with a friend.

Prayer

Lord, keep my heart on fire for You.
Help me not just feel faith, but live it every day. Amen.

Journal Prompt

What helps you keep your faith flame alive when it starts to fade?

A Heart of Gratitude

"Give thanks in all circumstances."

1 THESSALONIANS 5:18 (NIV)

STORY

After a tough year, Nala decided to write down one thing she was grateful for every night.

Some days, it was hard — all she could write was, *"I made it through today."*

But weeks later, flipping through her journal, she saw pages filled with blessings.

Gratitude had shifted her focus from what she lacked to what God had done.

INSIGHT

Gratitude doesn't change your situation — it changes your perspective.

Thankfulness reminds your heart that God is still good, even on the hard days.

> *"A grateful heart turns ordinary days into worship."*

ACTION STEP

Write or say three things you're thankful for before bed tonight.

PRAYER

Lord, thank You for all the blessings I overlook. Help me to live with gratitude every day. Amen.

JOURNAL PROMPT

What's one small thing you're grateful for today — and why does it matter?

Faith That Finishes Strong

*"I have fought the good fight,
I have finished the race,
I have kept the faith."*

2 TIMOTHY 4:7 (NIV)

STORY

During the last session of youth conference, the speaker said, "One day, you'll look back — make sure you can say,
'I finished strong.'"

Those words hit Jamila.

She didn't want to live half-hearted — she wanted her faith to last, even beyond youth group, even beyond feelings.

INSIGHT

Finishing strong isn't about never falling — it's about always rising.

A lasting faith isn't built in moments; it's built in a lifetime of yeses to God.

Keep walking. Keep trusting. Keep finishing well.

> *"Faith that lasts is faith that finishes."*

ACTION STEP

Reflect on your faith journey so far. Write down how God has carried you — and commit to staying the course.

PRAYER

God, thank You for walking with me this far.
Help me to keep running, keep trusting, and finish strong in You. Amen.

JOURNAL PROMPT

How do you want your faith to look years from now — and what can you do now to get there?

Faith in the Everyday

"Whatever you do,
do it all for the glory of God."

1 CORINTHIANS 10:31 (NIV)

STORY

Kara thought faith only counted during "spiritual" moments — church, worship, prayer.

Then her youth leader said, "Faith is how you treat people on a Monday morning."

That changed everything.

She started seeing God in her schoolwork, her chores, even her laughter. Faith wasn't just a feeling — it was a lifestyle.

Insight

Faith that lasts shows up in the ordinary.

God isn't waiting for you in perfect moments —
He's present in the daily ones.

How you live between Sundays says the most about
your faith.

> ## *"Real faith doesn't clock out after church."*

Action Step

Look for one moment today to glorify God — in kindness,
excellence, or attitude.

Prayer

Lord, help me live my faith every day, not just in certain
places.

Let everything I do reflect You. Amen.

Journal Prompt

Where can you invite God into your "ordinary" life this
week?

Faith That Walks in Love

*"Walk in the way of love,
just as Christ loved us."*

EPHESIANS 5:2 (NIV)

STORY

During lunch, a student sat alone every day.

Most people ignored her, but one day, Zara decided to sit with her.

They talked, laughed, and became friends.

Later, the girl said, "You made me feel seen."

That day, Zara learned love doesn't need a microphone — just a moment.

INSIGHT

Love is the heartbeat of lasting faith.

It's not just emotion — it's action.

When you walk in love, you carry Jesus into every conversation and every space.

> ### "If your faith doesn't move in love, it's standing still."

ACTION STEP

Show love through one intentional act of kindness today.

PRAYER

Jesus, help me love others like You do — with patience, compassion, and grace. Amen.

JOURNAL PROMPT

Who can you show love to today — especially someone who might not expect it?

Faith That Walks in Peace

"The peace of God, which transcends all understanding, will guard your hearts and your minds in Christ Jesus."

PHILIPPIANS 4:7 (NIV)

STORY

Josh's mind never stopped racing — exams, family, friends, the future.

One night, he played worship music quietly and just breathed.

The problems didn't vanish, but the panic lifted.

Peace wasn't the absence of chaos — it was the presence
of Christ.

INSIGHT

True peace isn't found in control; it's found in surrender.

When your heart is anchored in God, storms may come, but peace will stay.

> *"Peace isn't a place*
> *— it's a Person."*

ACTION STEP

Take five deep breaths and thank God for one thing after each. Feel His calm settle over you.

PRAYER

Lord, let Your peace fill my heart and guard my thoughts. Help me carry that peace wherever I go. Amen.

JOURNAL PROMPT

Where do you need peace most right now — and what helps you find it?

Faith That Walks in Humility

*"Humble yourselves before the Lord,
and he will lift you up."*

JAMES 4:10 (NIV)

STORY

Darren loved being right.

But after a heated debate with a friend, he realised pride was blocking peace.

He apologised, even though it bruised his ego.

That night, he felt lighter. Winning had felt good — but humility felt holy.

INSIGHT

Humility isn't thinking less of yourself — it's thinking of yourself less.

When you walk humbly, you leave more room for God's grace to shine through you.

"Pride shouts; humility whispers — and God hears the whisper."

ACTION STEP

Do something kind today without seeking credit or praise.

PRAYER

Lord, help me walk humbly before You.
Let my confidence come from grace, not pride. Amen.

JOURNAL PROMPT

Where is pride hardest to let go — and what would humility look like there?

Faith That Walks in Forgiveness

"Forgive as the Lord forgave you."

COLOSSIANS 3:13 (NIV)

STORY

Naomi carried anger for months after a friend betrayed her.

Then during worship, she felt God whisper, *"You can't hold grace with closed fists."*

She cried, forgave, and felt free.

Forgiveness didn't excuse what happened — it released her heart from it.

INSIGHT

Unforgiveness poisons peace.

Forgiveness doesn't make the other person right — it makes your heart right.

When you forgive, you mirror Jesus more clearly.

> *"Forgiveness isn't saying it's okay — it's saying I'm free."*

ACTION STEP

Think of one person you need to forgive. Pray for them, even if it's hard.

PRAYER

God, thank You for forgiving me.

Help me release bitterness and walk free in Your grace. Amen.

JOURNAL PROMPT

Who do you need to forgive — and how could that decision free your heart today?

Faith That Walks in Purpose

*"We are God's masterpiece,
created in Christ Jesus
to do good works."*

EPHESIANS 2:10 (NLT)

STORY

Toby often felt like he didn't matter.

Then one youth service, the leader said, "You're not an accident — you're an assignment."

That hit deep.

He started volunteering, using his creativity to serve, and discovered purpose wasn't about spotlight — it was about service.

Insight

You were made on purpose, for a purpose.

When you live that truth, even small actions carry eternal meaning.

> *"You're not random —*
> *you're handcrafted for impact."*

Action Step

Ask God to show you one way you can use your gifts to make a difference this week.

Prayer

Lord, thank You for creating me with purpose.
Help me use my gifts to serve and glorify You.
Amen.

Journal Prompt

What's something you're passionate about that could become a way to serve God?

Faith That Walks in Joy

"The joy of the Lord is your strength."

NEHEMIAH 8:10 (NIV)

STORY

During a rough season, Aiden still smiled — not fake, but real.

His friends asked, "Why are you always so positive?"

He said, "Because joy doesn't depend on what's happening — it depends on Who's with me."

Joy had become his strength.

Insight

Happiness depends on circumstances; joy depends on Christ.

Even when life feels heavy, joy reminds your soul that God is still good.

> *"Joy isn't what happens to you — it's what God builds in you."*

Action Step

Do something joyful today — worship, laugh, or encourage someone else.

Prayer

Lord, fill me with joy that no circumstance can steal. Let it be my strength and my song. Amen.

Journal Prompt

What brings you joy in God — and how can you protect that joy daily?

Faith That Walks in Courage

"Be strong and courageous.
Do not be afraid;
do not be discouraged."

JOSHUA 1:9 (NIV)

STORY

Serena feared speaking up about her beliefs at school.

But one day, when a classmate mocked Christianity, she gently said, "That's not what Jesus is about."

The room went quiet.

She was scared, but peaceful — courage had spoken louder than fear.

INSIGHT

Courage doesn't mean you never feel afraid; it means you move forward despite it.

When God calls you to stand, He also stands with you.

> *"Courage isn't the absence of fear*
> *— it's faith on its feet."*

ACTION STEP

Stand for truth or kindness today — even if it feels uncomfortable.

PRAYER

Lord, fill me with courage to live boldly for You.
Help me trust Your strength when I feel weak.
Amen.

JOURNAL PROMPT

What's one area of your life that needs more courage right now?

Faith That Walks in Faithfulness

"His master replied, 'Well done, good and faithful servant.'"

MATTHEW 25:21 (NIV)

STORY

Kofi didn't think his small acts mattered — stacking chairs, welcoming people, tidying up.

But his leader said, "Faithfulness in small things prepares you for big ones."

That truth stuck.

Years later, Kofi realised consistency builds legacy.

Insight

Faithfulness isn't about fame — it's about stewardship.

God sees your quiet obedience and rewards it openly.

Keep showing up; heaven notices.

> *"Faithfulness is doing little things with big love."*

Action Step

Be faithful today in something small — even if no one sees it.

Prayer

Lord, thank You for noticing every act of faithfulness. Help me keep serving with a humble heart. Amen.

Journal Prompt

What's one small area where you can be more consistent for God?

Faith That Walks in Wonder

"Stand still and consider the wondrous works of God."

JOB 37:14 (KJV)

STORY

During a hike, Layla stopped to look at the sunset.

The sky was a mix of gold and pink — breathtaking.

In that quiet moment, she felt awe — not of nature alone, but of the God who painted it.

She whispered, "You're amazing."

Insight

Faith that lasts keeps its sense of wonder.

When you pause to notice God's beauty in creation, kindness, and grace, your heart stays alive to His presence.

> *"Wonder keeps faith*
> *from growing cold."*

Action Step

Take a moment today to marvel at something God made — and thank Him for it.

Prayer

Lord, don't let me lose my sense of wonder.
Help me see Your hand in the ordinary and the extraordinary. Amen.

Journal Prompt

When was the last time you felt truly amazed by God — and what caused it?

Faith That Walks On

*"The one who stands firm
to the end will be saved."*

MATTHEW 24:13 (NIV)

STORY

On the last day of youth camp, the leader said,
"This isn't the end — it's the start."

Those words stayed with Sienna as she packed her
bag and faced normal life again.

Faith wasn't just for campfires and songs — it was
for classrooms, challenges, and choices ahead.

Insight

Faith that lasts doesn't end with a season — it carries on into every one.

It's not a sprint; it's a lifelong walk with Jesus.

Keep walking — because He's walking with you.

"Faith doesn't finish at the end
— it walks on."

Action Step

Thank God for the growth this journey has brought — and ask Him for strength for the next one.

Prayer

Jesus, thank You for walking with me every day. Help me keep going, keep growing, and keep shining for You. Amen.

Journal Prompt

What has changed in your faith over these 90 days — and how will you keep walking with God from here?

Set Apart to Shine

THEME RECAP

This month focused on living differently — rooted in truth, walking in grace, and finishing strong. You've learned that being set apart isn't about perfection; it's about purpose.

REFLECT

1. Where do you see growth in your faith journey since January?

2. What does "living set apart" mean to you now?

3. How will you keep your fire for God burning beyond this devotional?

Pray

Jesus, thank You for walking with me through these 90 days. Keep me rooted, bold, and burning bright for You. Let my faith continue to grow long after these pages. Amen.

Action

Write a personal "Faith on Fire Commitment" — a paragraph capturing what you've learned and how you'll live it out. Share it with a friend, mentor, or youth leader.

EXPLORE THE COMPLETE SERIES

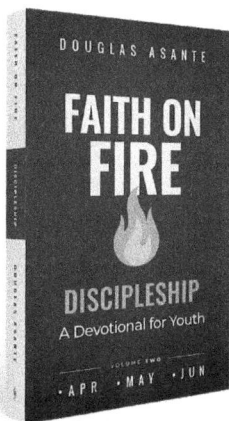

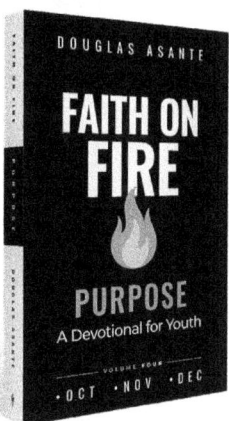

DOUGLAS ASANTE

FAITH ON FIRE

IDENTITY
A Devotional for Youth

VOLUME ONE
· JAN · FEB · MAR

DOUGLAS ASANTE

FAITH ON FIRE

DISCIPLESHIP
A Devotional for Youth

VOLUME TWO
· APR · MAY · JUN

DOUGLAS ASANTE

FAITH ON FIRE

RELATIONSHIPS
A Devotional for Youth

VOLUME THREE
· JUL · AUG · SEP

DOUGLAS ASANTE

FAITH ON FIRE

PURPOSE
A Devotional for Youth

VOLUME FOUR
· OCT · NOV · DEC

AVAILABLE ON

amazon   amazon kindle

www.ingramcontent.com/pod-product-compliance
Lightning Source LLC
Chambersburg PA
CBHW060238050426
42448CB00009B/1497